D1245117

IDEA LAB

Niki Ahrens

Lerner Publications ◆ Minneapolis

To Ms. Erin Becerra, Ms. Flo Yssel, and Ms. Rachel Finney, who inspire innovation in STEAM by seeing and loving children first

Lerner Publications Company
A division of Lerner Publishing Group, Inc.
241 First Avenue North
Minneapolis, MN 55401 USA

For reading levels and more information, look up this title at www.lernerbooks.com.

Main body text set in Mikado a 14/18.
Typeface provided by HVD Fonts.

Library of Congress Cataloging-in-Publication Data

Names: Ahrens, Niki, 1979– author.
Title: Big Hero 6 idea lab / Niki Ahrens.
Other titles: Big Hero six idea lab
Description: Minneapolis : Lerner Publications, [2020] | Series: Disney STEAM projects | Includes bibliographical references and index. | Audience: Ages 7–11. | Audience: Grade 4 to 6.
Identifiers: LCCN 2018050613 (print) | LCCN 2018051945 (ebook) | ISBN 9781541561557 (eb pdf) | ISBN 9781541554825 (lb : alk. paper)
Subjects: LCSH: Handicraft—Juvenile literature. | Science projects—Juvenile literature. | Superheroes—Juvenile literature. | Big Hero 6 (Motion picture)—Juvenile literature.
Classification: LCC TT160 (ebook) | LCC TT160 .A33 2020 (print) | DDC 745.5—dc23

LC record available at https://lccn.loc.gov/2018050613

Manufactured in the United States of America
1-45800-42682-2/15/2019

Contents

The Incredible Teamwork of *Big Hero 6*

Hiro and the Big Hero 6 team create clever inventions to protect San Fransokyo. They build robots, mix up strange chemistry experiments, and work with powerful lasers in their lab to become high-tech crime-fighting team. Supervillains don't stand a chance!

Explore San Fransokyo and the world of *Big Hero 6* with fun science, technology, engineering, art, and math projects.

Before You Get Started

Each project lists materials you will need. Ask an adult to help you gather the materials at home, from a craft or hardware store, or online. To keep your workspace clean, cover it with newspaper or cardboard before you begin. And when you finish each project, be sure to clean up your work area.

Ask an adult for permission and help with sharp tools. Be careful when using scissors. And have fun with the Big Hero 6 team!

Cityscape Array

Big Hero 6 must save San Fransokyo from Yokai. Use your design skills to create a San Fransokyo cityscape.

Materials
- pencil
- construction paper in at least 2 different colors
- ruler
- scissors
- glue stick
- pair of dice (optional)
- markers

1. Draw tall city buildings in different shapes and sizes on construction paper. A ruler can help you make straight lines. Cut out the buildings.

2. Glue the buildings in a row on a large sheet of construction paper of a different color.

3. Cut at least four small squares of construction paper. The squares should be a different color from the buildings.

4. Glue the squares onto a building in an array. An array is objects arranged in rows and columns. For example, a 2 × 2 array would have two rows of windows with two columns in each row.

5. Choose different arrays for the other buildings. Try rolling two dice to get the row and column numbers for the arrays. Cut out more small paper windows, and glue them to the buildings.

6. San Fransokyo was inspired by Tokyo and San Francisco. Use the two real cities as inspiration to add designs to your San Fransokyo cityscape with markers. You can hang it up in your room like a poster!

Go Go Tomago Spinner

Go Go Tomago fights evil with fast-spinning discs. You can design a colorful disc that will spin on a looped string.

Materials
- pencil
- drinking glass
- cardboard
- scissors
- markers
- hole punch (optional)
- string

1. Use a pencil to trace a circle around a drinking glass on a piece of cardboard. Cut out the circle. This will be your spinning disc.

2. Use markers to decorate the disc with colorful designs.

1.

3. Carefully use the pencil or hole punch to make two holes near the center of the disc, about ½ inch (1.2 cm) apart.

4. Cut a piece of string 36 inches (0.9 m) long.

2a.

5. Thread one end of the string through both punched holes. Then tie the ends of the string together, forming a loop.

6. Hold one end of the loop in each hand with the disc in the center. Twist the looped string by making small, quick circles with your hands in the same direction. The string should start twisting on either side of the disc.

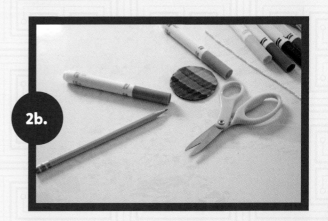
2b.

7. When the string is twisted almost all the way to your hands, repeat stretching your hands apart and bringing them together. If the string is twisted tightly, the disc will spin like a fan.

8. When your string unwinds, repeat steps 6 and 7 and try again.

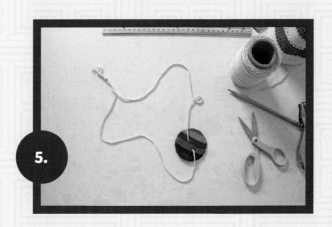
5.

Mixed-Up Goo

Mix up a playful substance like one that Honey Lemon might create in the lab.

Materials
- 1 cup water
- large bowl
- 2 cups cornstarch
- food coloring
- spoon (optional)

1. Slowly pour the water into the bowl.

2. Carefully add the cornstarch to the water.

3. Add 2 to 3 drops of food coloring to the water and cornstarch mixture.

4. Use a spoon or your hands to stir the mixture gently to form goo.

5. Pick up the goo. Does it stay together like a solid or spread out like a liquid? Next, roll the goo into a ball and see if it acts like a solid or a liquid. Try different things to see how the goo reacts.

STEAM Takeaway

The mixed-up goo is a non-Newtonian fluid. Non-Newtonian fluids can behave like liquids or solids depending on the forces acting on them. When the goo is at rest, it behaves like a liquid. When a force such as the motion created by your hands acts on the goo, it behaves like a solid.

Magnetic Sculpture

Hiro's microbots join together to form useful structures. Use metal parts and magnets instead of microbots to build a sculpture.

Materials
- metal lid from a jam or mason jar
- 4 to 6 hobby magnets
- 10 to 15 nuts, bolts, and washers
- a few paper clips or small metal pieces

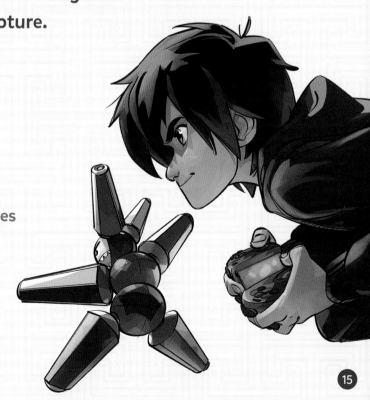

1. Set the metal lid on a tabletop.

2. Attach a hobby magnet to the surface of the lid.

3. Place nuts, bolts, washers, and other metal bits, such as paper clips, on the magnet to create a sculpture.

4. Add more magnets to make the sculpture taller or wider.

5. Continue to add metal bits around the magnets to create a design that you like. You can make your sculpture stand tall or spread it out along the lid.

STEAM Takeaway

A sculpture is a form of 3-D art. A relief sculpture projects from a background and often hangs on a wall. A sculpture in the round stands freely on a base, like many statues. Your magnetic sculpture can be relief or a sculpture in the round depending on how you build and display it.

Jumping Magnets

Go Go Tomago uses magnetic force to move high-speed wheels. You can use the same force to make magnets jump and move without touching them.

Materials
- drinking straw
- clothespin
- 3 or more disc magnets with holes

1. **Place the straw upright on a table or countertop. Clip the clothespin to the bottom of the straw, and grasp the clothespin to hold the straw in place.**

2. **With your other hand, place one disc magnet onto the straw so it slides down.**

3. **Add another disc magnet to the straw. If the top magnet attaches to the bottom magnet, remove the top magnet and turn it over. Flipping it turns its magnetic poles. Drop it onto the straw again. The magnets will push away from each other instead of pull together.**

1.

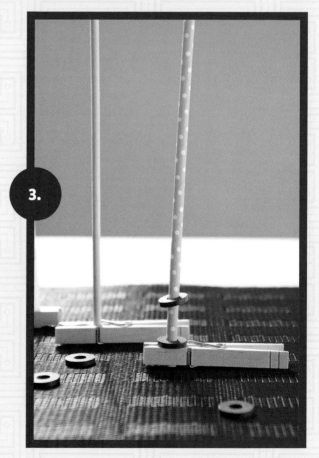

3.

4. Slide the bottom magnet up the straw, and watch the top magnet move without anything touching it.

5. You can add more magnets to the straw and watch how they jump and move when you slide the bottom magnet upward.

5.

STEAM Takeaway

Magnets have a north pole and a south pole. The pole of one magnet is attracted to the opposite pole of another and pushes away from the same pole. So a magnet's north pole is attracted to the south pole of another magnet, but two north poles push away from each other.

Lemon Balloon

Honey Lemon uses chemical reactions to help make the world a better place. Chemistry can help you use a lemon to inflate a balloon.

Materials

- kitchen funnel
- empty plastic water bottle
- 3 ounces (⅓ cup) lemon juice
- uninflated balloon
- 2 tablespoons baking soda

1. Hold the kitchen funnel above the water bottle, and pour the lemon juice.

2. Rinse and dry the funnel.

3. Hold the balloon so its opening is facing upward, and place the narrow end of the funnel in the opening. Pour the baking soda into the funnel, allowing the baking soda to fall into the balloon.

4. Making sure you keep the baking soda in the balloon, carefully wrap the opening of the balloon around the lemon juice bottle's opening.

5. Slowly tip the balloon up to allow the baking soda to fall into the bottle and mix with the lemon juice.

6. Watch the balloon inflate!

STEAM Takeaway

Lemon juice mixed with baking soda causes a chemical reaction. When they interact in the bottle, they create a gas called carbon dioxide. This gas inflates the balloon.

Bouncing Bubbles

Baymax the personal health-care robot can bounce. Blow bubbles that bounce on your hand.

Materials
- 1 cup distilled water
- bowl
- 3 ounces (⅓ cup) liquid dish soap
- drinking straw or pipe cleaner
- 1 teaspoon shampoo
- knit winter glove

1. Pour the distilled water into a bowl.

2. Add the dish soap, and gently stir with your straw or pipe cleaner.

3. Add the shampoo to the water to help the bubbles last longer.

4. Put a knit winter glove on one hand.

5. If you're using a straw, dip one end of the straw into the liquid. Gently blow a bubble through the dry end of the straw. If you have a pipe cleaner instead, shape an end of the pipe cleaner into a dime-size circle. Twist the end to seal the circle, and dip it into the liquid. Gently blow a bubble through the circle.

6. Try to catch the bubble on your gloved hand. The glove's soft fabric allows the bubble to bounce.

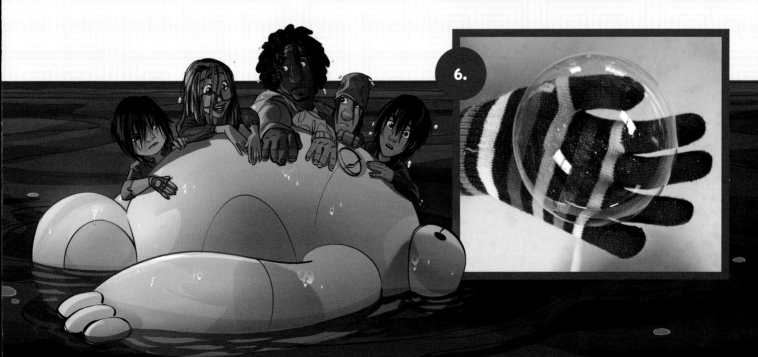

Laser Rainbow

Wasabi uses lasers to make precise slices. Point a flashlight like a laser, and use it to create a rainbow light show.

Materials
- clear glass jar
- water
- flashlight
- reused compact disc (CD)
- masking tape

1. Fill the glass jar halfway with water. Set the jar on a surface near a wall.

2. Hold the flashlight so the handle is parallel with the wall. Point the flashlight at the jar so light shines through the water and out the opposite side. Set the flashlight down, leaving the light on to shine through the jar.

3. Lean the CD against the opposite side of the jar from the flashlight, so it faces the flashlight. Angle the CD until a rainbow appears on the wall. Tape the CD to the jar to hold it in place.

4. Try making new rainbow designs by adjusting the positions of the jar, flashlight, and CD.

STEAM Takeaway

Tiny ridges on the CD cause light to split into different colors, forming a rainbow. Water causes light to bend, which also separates the colors and forms a rainbow.

Solar Oven

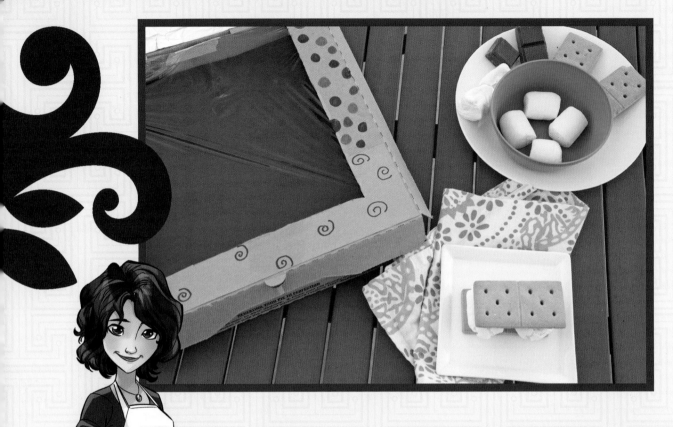

Aunt Cass makes delicious food at the Lucky Cat Café. You can build an oven that heats food using the sun's energy.

Materials

- shallow cardboard box like a clean pizza box
- markers
- ruler
- scissors
- glue stick
- aluminum foil
- black construction paper
- clear plastic wrap
- masking tape
- marshmallows
- 2 sticks
- graham crackers
- chocolate bar

1. Place the closed box with its hinge facing away from you. Start near the back-left corner, and draw a long line 1 to 2 inches (2.5 to 5 cm) from the box's edge. Keep going until you draw three sides of a rectangle, stopping near the back-right corner.

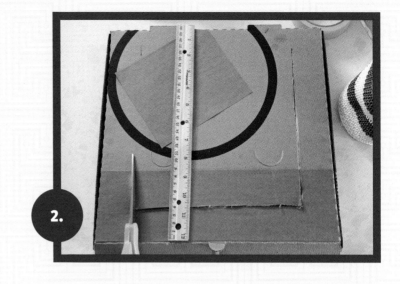

2. With an adult's help, cut along the line to create a door flap.

3. Decorate the outside of the box with markers.

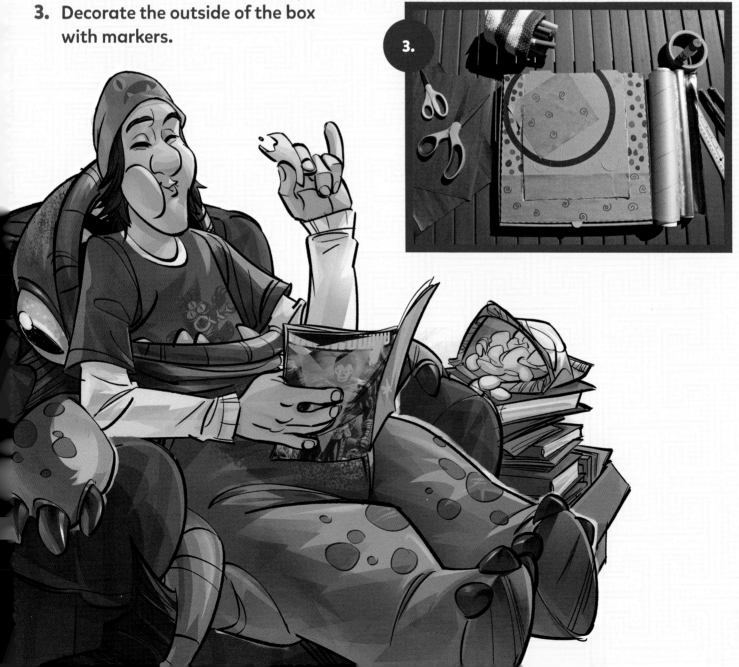

4.

6.

4. Glue a sheet of aluminum foil, with the shinier side facing up, to the inside of the door flap.

5. Glue a sheet of black construction paper to the inside bottom of the box.

6. Stretch clear plastic wrap across the door flap's opening, and tape it in place. Your solar oven is ready!

7. Place a few marshmallows inside the oven near the middle of the black paper, and close the box top.

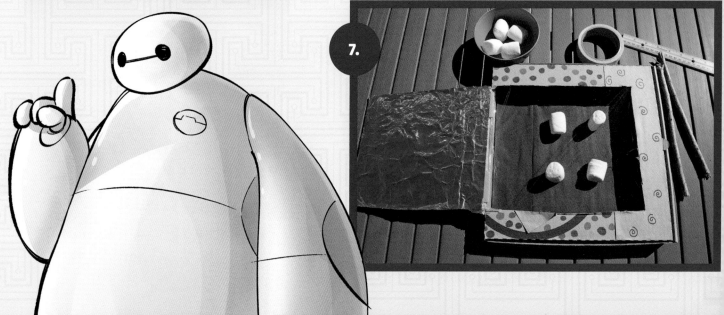

7.

8. Take your oven to an unshaded space outside. Make sure it is a warm and sunny day! Set your oven to face the sun, and prop the door flap open with sticks at the sides. Adjust the flap and sticks until the aluminum foil reflects sunlight into the box. Then tape the sticks in place.

9. Wait 1 to 2 hours for the marshmallows to heat up. Try serving them between two graham crackers with a small piece of chocolate to make s'mores.

9.

STEAM Takeaway

Solar ovens work by focusing heat from the sun. Aluminum foil reflects sunlight into the box that is absorbed by the black paper. The paper heats up and warms the air above it. Plastic wrap traps the warm air in the box, heating the marshmallows. Yum!

Glossary

array: objects arranged in rows and columns

chemical reaction: when two or more chemicals interact to create a new substance

cityscape: an artistic image of a city

magnetism: a force that can attract and repel

non-Newtonian fluid: a substance that can behave as a solid or a liquid

parallel: lying in the same direction without meeting

sculpture: a 3-D work of art

3-D: something that has height, width, and depth

To Learn More

Books

Heinecke, Liz Lee. *STEAM Lab for Kids: 52 Creative Hands-On Projects for Exploring Science, Technology, Engineering, Art, and Math*. Beverly, MA: Quarry Books, 2018. Try more fun STEAM projects.

Thompson, Veronica. *Earth-Friendly Engineering Crafts*. Minneapolis: Lerner Publications, 2019. Transform your family's recycled materials into fun and useful treasures.

Websites

12 Things You Didn't Know about *Big Hero 6*
https://ohmy.disney.com/movies/2015/02/18/9-things-you-didnt-know
-about-big-hero-6/
See movie images and learn more about *Big Hero 6*.

Let's Take a Day Trip to San Fransokyo
https://ohmy.disney.com/movies/2016/12/14/lets-take-a-day-trip-to
-san-fransokyo/
Visit San Fransokyo at this fun website.

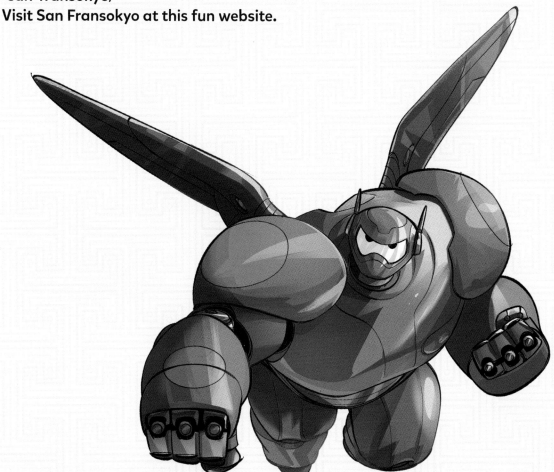

Index

Photo Acknowledgments

Additional image credits: Belozersky/Shutterstock.com (flask); E_K/Shutterstock.com (gears); Aksenova Natalya/Shutterstock.com p. 6 (glue); Olga Kovalenko/Shutterstock.com, p. 6 (scissors); Gina Djumlija/EyeEm/Getty Images, p. 7 (paper); SJ Travel Photo and Video/Shutterstock.com, p. 7 (paints).

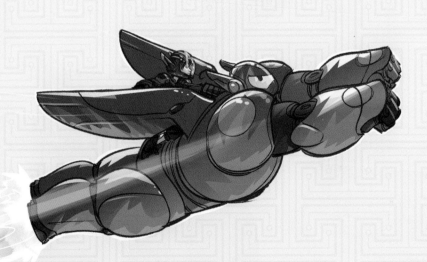